MULTIPLICANDO

By Howard Schrager

Other Works by Howard Schrager
&

Lemon Tree Press

Currently available:

LMNOP and All the Letters A to Z
Working with LMNOP
A Manual for Parents and Teachers

LMNOP Alphabet Wall Cards

King Maximo & the Number Knights
Sarah & the Number Knights
A Knife and a Fork and a Bottle and a Cork
Rock Forms
Song of the Rain-California's Water Cycle

ISBN-13: 978 0 9644846 8 0

Copyright © 2019 Howard Schrager ∞ LemonTree Press

All rights reserved. No part of this publication may be copied or reprinted without permission from the author and publisher. For more information about permission to reproduce selections from this book write LemonTree Press, PO Box 1709, Monterey, California 93940 howardschrager@lmntreepress.com
www.lmntreepress.com

For James and Julius
and the one to come...

with thanks to Malin, Zoe, and Soren

Note to Parents and Teachers

During over thirty years of teaching I have seen it confirmed, time and again, that young children have far more of a feeling and imaginative nature than they are little thinkers. The heart is the gateway to a child's mind and the story is the gateway to the heart. In play and in artistic work children integrate their experiences. To be able to learn in a playful, imaginative way, appropriate to their stage of development, cultivates and quickens the children's capacities, and lays the basis for the subsequent development of an intellect imbued with creative force.
From the introduction to WORKING WITH LMNOP

Multiplicando is a teaching story, an introduction to multiplication in its relation to other mathematical processes. It covers a key piece of the math curriculum, but, perhaps more importantly, it is intended to connect and integrate children's imaginative, physical and feeling life with their math learning experience. If we prove successful we will certainly find the children to have enthusiasm for future math learning.

Unlike many stories, Multiplicando is not meant to be read all at once. Ideally it would be told in a series of lessons extending over several weeks, presented in conjunction with movement and artistic activities, as well as practice in the math processes involved. Teaching in this way presents a special opportunity to bring math teaching into the creative realm, with the wealth of potential benefits that this entails. Before beginning to tell the story, please be sure to look in the back of the book where you will find a special section "Using Multiplicando."

Howard Schrager
Monterey, California
July 2019

TABLE OF CONTENTS

MULTIPLICANDO ... 1

GUS PLUS ... 3

THE TOWER ROOM ... 5

TODD & STEVEN ... 8

TWOS ... 10

THAT NIGHT ... 12

THE SIGN OF MULTIPLICANDO ... 13

THREES ... 14

FOURS ... 16

THE SIGN OF KING DIVIDE ... 18

WHAT RODERICK TOLD THEM ... 21

WHICH THINGS COME IN WHATS ... 22

SHARE FAIR AND SQUARE ... 24

HER HIGHNESS MINUS ... 26

GIVING AWAY IN A FAST WAY ... 27

CHECKING ... 29

DOUBLE THREES ... 31

DOUBLE FOURS, TRIPLE THREES ... 32

WAYS OF SAYING ... 36

ROSEMARY DREAMS ELEVEN ... 37

SAME WITH 12s JUST A LITTLE DIFFERENT ... 39

MULTIPLICANDO'S TABLE ... 40

USING MULTIPLICANDO

Multiplicando

Multiplicando walked lightly along the path that followed the stream through the dense forest. The sun, high in the sky, filtered in through the leaves, and birds were singing everywhere. Multiplicando was feeling fine. Suddenly he turned three back flips in a row, and then while keeping the beat with his feet, step- step-leap, step-step-leap, he began to recite...

>Here am I
>'Neath the trees
>The blue sky
>Over me
>I feel fine
>And so free
>The good king
>Shall I see
>And the queen
>Queen Hellene
>La la la
>La la la...

The forest opened up a bit, and Multiplicando could see in the distance the towers of a castle, its flags flying in the breeze. He breathed in the good air of the day and thought about how wonderful it would be to be at the castle after his long journey. After a time he came to a ford in the stream. He bent over and scooped up some water to cool his face, when he saw his reflection. "Look!" he said, "There's the magician, mathematician." Then he noticed something else. It was the stepping stones he had laid out in the stream the last time he'd been by that way.

The stones were arranged in a repeating pattern across the stream with two small ones and then one large.
"Here I go!" he said, and he crossed the stream—
step-step-leap, step-step-leap—landing on the larger stones with his feet spread-eagled.

GUS PLUS

Multiplicando stood before the east gate of the castle. The guard greeted him cheerfully and let him pass. Quietly he slipped into the bakery, inhaling the warm scents. There, standing over a huge baking pan, stood a stout, red-faced baker all in white. Multiplicando tip-toed up behind him, and, in a loud whisper, called out, "Good Gus, how goes it with us." The good-natured baker, only slightly startled, replied slowly, "Why Multiplicando, where have you been?

"Oh, you know, between here and there. I've missed you, Gus. And, I must say, I've also missed your tarts. Do you think I could have one?" he said pointing.

"Sure, go ahead, but listen my friend, do you suppose you could come back later. I'm having a tough time coming up with the right number of tarts for the king's feast tonight. It's always the same. I keep losing track. See here, 2 and 2 is 4, and 3 more is 7, and 5 more is 12, and 6 more is 18, and … and … and … that's where I lose count. I just get confused."

"Well," said Multiplicando, "I can see you are fine at adding. One could call you 'Gus Plus' for that matter. Here's my solution. See how you have them laid out every which way. Why don't you lay them out like the five-card in the king's deck—two above, two below, and one in the middle?"

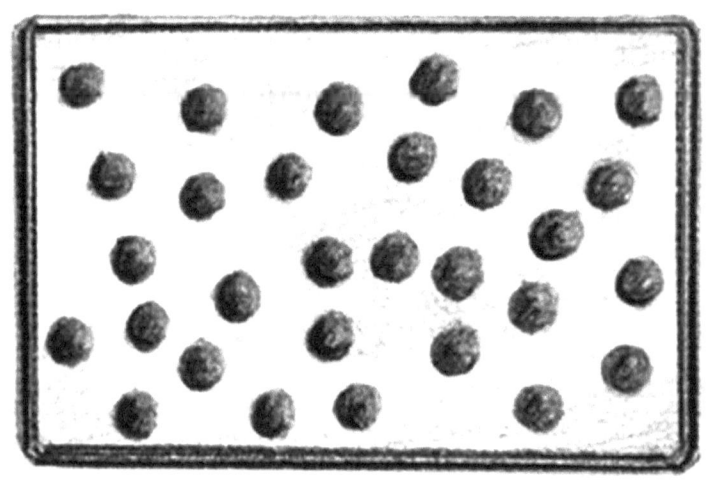

Reaching over the baking sheet and rearranging the tarts Multiplicando said, "There, now all you have to do is count the ones in the middle, and count by fives as you do. You know, the way you counted for games when you were a boy."

"Oh, you mean 5, 10, 15, 20…?" replied Gus.

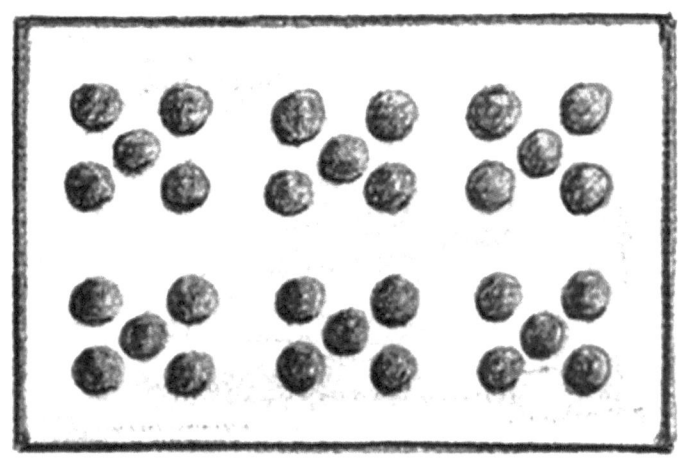

"Yeah, that's it!" said Multiplicando. And Multiplicando did six cartwheels in the bakery, just like that. After the first he counted FIVE—after the second he counted TEN—after the third he counted FIFTEEN—and so on. "There, that's 5 six times, or, as I like to say, 6 times 5 is 30," said Multiplicando, standing there spread-eagled, with a big smile on his face. "Got It Gus?"

"Yes," said the baker, "methinks I do," and a broad grin spread across his face.

TOWER ROOM

The king and queen were overjoyed to see Multiplicando, and the twins, Raymond and Rosemary, rushed up to greet him. "King Divide, Your Highness Minus, "said Multiplicando bowing low.

"What did he call Mommy and Daddy?" whispered Raymond to Rosemary.

"I think he called them 'King Divide' and 'Your Highness Minus', whatever in the world that means," Rosemary whispered back.

The queen, overhearing them, said, "Dear children this is a joke between Multiplicando and us. He can do no wrong in our eyes. You see, it was he who brought us the 'Golden Scale' and the 'Table of Multiplicando'."

"The Golden Scale?" exclaimed the two at the same time.

"Well, you are probably too young to remember, but old enough now to understand," said their mother laughing. "Multiplicando, would you be good enough to show these two to the Tower Room."

"Yes, Your Highness," answered Multiplicando, bowing low.

"The Tower Room!" said Raymond excitedly. "Father always said that we could go there when we were nine. Now here we are, going with Multiplicando!"

Multiplicando turned the key in the tower door and pushed it open. In the center of the small room stood a table with a golden scale upon it, which gleamed in the sunlight that streamed in through the lone window. "This is the Golden Scale," pronounced Multiplicando.

Multiplicando poured a purse full of gold coins onto the table. "Watch carefully," he said, placing some coins onto the left-hand tray. The tray went down, while the other swung upward.

"It's like a seesaw," Raymond remarked, "but I want it to balance the way it did when it was empty."

"Okay," said Multiplicando, "let's see what we can do. Let's put some coins on the right-hand tray."

"Still doesn't balance," called out Raymond.

"Let's take a look," said Multiplicando. "How many are in the left hand tray?"
"Eight," replied Rosemary immediately.

"Now, how many do we have in the right hand tray, Raymond?"
"Five," replied Raymond.

"So, Rosemary, how many more coins will it take to balance the scales?"

"Three more, I think."

"Correcto! Now why is that? You see, if I gave you 8 nuts and Raymond only five, he would say that was not fair. So to be the same, or 'equal' as a mathematician likes to say, I'd have to give Raymond three more, wouldn't I? Would it be fair to say that 8 is 5 and 3?"

Multiplicando added three coins to the lighter side, and the twins watched the Golden Scale find its balance again.

"Now here's the best part," said Multiplicando. "One day as your mother, father and I were experimenting with the Golden Scale, we wanted to write down something to show that both sides are the same, or equal, when the trays are balanced. Your mother noticed that the crossbar went straight across when the trays balanced, so she suggested that we use the sign of the crossbar to show that both sides were the same. Because mathematicians like to do things the shortest way possible, I suggested we draw two short lines to stand for the crossbar, to show an 'equals' sign because equals means 'the same as'. So in this instance we can write $8 = 5 + 3$.

$$8 = 5 + 3$$

Suddenly, there came a knock on the door. It was a servant informing them that it was time to dress for the birthday feast. As they turned to go, Rosemary noticed that there was an unusual pattern on the table, but what it was?

"Hurry, we must not be late for the feast!" said Multiplicando. Rosemary's question would have to wait.

TODD AND STEVEN

The great birthday feast was held, and what a feast it was! Aside from all the wonderful food, there were sword swallowers, belly dancers, and best of all, Multiplicando performing his greatest feat, turning cartwheels while juggling four balls.

The next morning at breakfast, seeing Raymond looking quite thoughtful, Multiplicando asked, "What's on your mind, young sir?"

"Well, I can't get it out of my mind how strangely the serving boys, Todd and Steven, were acting," said Raymond. "Each time people sat down at a table, it was almost as if they would have a little squabble."

"Oh-h-h-h-h," said Multiplicando, "do you know what they were doing? Whenever an odd number of people were seated at a table, Todd would wait on them. If there was an even number, Steven would take care of them. It's a kind of game they play."

"What do you mean, 'odd', Multiplicando?"

"Well, you know the custom in your land whereby people always sit across from people who are at the table? They pair up, even if they don't know each other."

"If they can," added Rosemary, "unless there is an extra one, then that's the odd one."

"Correcto!" said Multiplicando.

For several days afterwards Raymond and Rosemary enjoyed playing the game they called *Todd and Steven's Inn*. They would have a certain number of their friends sit down at a table. Then they would say,

Todd and Steven,

Odd or Even,

Tell Me If It's

Odd or Even

If there was going to be an even number, such as 2, 4, 6, 8 or 10, for example, then Steven would wait on the table. If there was going to be an odd number such as 1, 3, 5, 7, 9 or 11, then Todd would wait on them.

"It somehow seems that it is easier for Steven," said Rosemary.

"I think I know why," said her brother proudly. When they're seated in pairs you just count by 2's. With the odds there's always that extra one you have to add, the odd one."

"It's definitely easier to count the evens," said Rosemary. "But not that much harder with the odds," added Raymond.

Even & Even, that's for Steven.

Even & Odd, that's for Todd.

Odd & Odd, that's for Steven.

TWOs

Raymond and Rosemary were looking down from the battlements onto the court yard at the palace guards, marching back and forth.

"There's is something about their marching I have never noticed before. What is it?" Raymond wondered aloud.

"I know," said Rosemary, "The Captain is keeping time with his baton and the guards are all stamping hard on the right foot. Listen to the way it sounds. 1 **2** 3 **4** 5 **6** 7 **8** 9 **10** 11 **12**. "

The twins kept the rhythm on the stone wall, clapping on the even beat.

        Tap CLAP

        Tap CLAP

        Tap CLAP

        Tap CLAP

They even practiced marching like the guards, stamping hard on the evens.

Multiplicando was practicing cartwheels in the courtyard when they found him. "So, it looks like you've discovered the 2's table while you were playing, eh?"

"The 2's table?" questioned Raymond. "What do you mean by that?" "Well, never mind the table part for now… Let's count by twos."

"That's easy for us," said Rosemary. "We're twins, and we do everything by two. Try us."

"Okay, each time I do a cartwheel, that's two more. Got it?" "Sure, let's go," said Raymond.

Multiplicando turned one cartwheel. "TWO!" shouted the twins. Then Multiplicando turned another. "FOUR!" they cried out together, and another, "SIX!"

Now he turned 4 cartwheels.

"EIGHT," they called out. "And as Multiplicando continued, the twins counted "… 10, 12, 14, 16, 18, 20, 22…"

"Last one," called Multiplicando, "24," was the reply.

"Good work, you two," said Multiplicando.

THAT NIGHT

That night when they were in their room, Raymond asked Rosemary, "How much is it when you count 2, four times?"

"4 times 2 is 8."

"6 times 2?" he asked.

"12," she answered. "6 times 2 is 12. It's easy. I can see the people at the big tables seated opposite each other in pairs. If I count the people on one side, then I know how many pairs there are, and I count by twos. It's starting to make sense."

"Okay, Rose, now you give me some." "7 times 2?"

"7 times 2 is ... let's see ... 14. Another, please." "8 times 2?"

"8 times 2 is 16. You know, Rose, I can feel the twos adding up in my mind. And, I can still feel Multiplicando doing his cartwheels."

They were so excited they couldn't sleep.   "You know, Raymond, I can't stop thinking about Multiplicando."

"Neither can I, Rose! Where's the slate? I've just got to draw a picture of him." He did, and in just a few moments they were sound asleep.

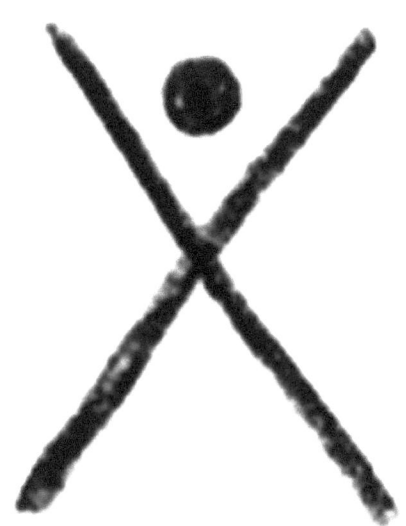

THE SIGN OF MULTIPLICANDO

The next evening, Rosemary had an idea. She took her slate and started writing. When she'd finished she called Raymond over.

"See here, these numbers were just waiting for me to put them in order. I just thought it would be nice to use Multiplicando's picture when we say 'times'. Of course, not the whole picture, just a sign, like mathematicians do."

Then she recited what she'd written.

```
2  is 1 × 2        14 is 7 × 2
4  is 2 × 2        16 is 8 × 2
6  is 3 × 2        18 is 9 × 2
8  is 4 × 2        20 is 10 × 2
10 is 5 × 2        22 is 11 × 2
12 is 6 × 2        24 is 12 × 2
```

THREEs

"Rose, did you ever watch the way Multiplicando sometimes goes through the halls reciting rhymes as he goes? He takes two steps and then does a little leap."

"Yes, I have," said Rosemary. "Maybe we can make a rhyme too." She pondered a minute, and then started stepping like Multiplicando, step-step-leap, step-step-leap. Raymond followed along. While they were stepping Rosemary started to recite,

> "Now I skip
> Merrily
> With no cares
> Feeling free
> And my feet
> Fairly fly
> I'm a bird
> In the sky ..."

"Now, Rose, don't get carried away!"

That night while she was writing numbers on her slate by candlelight, Rosemary decided to write out the numbers according to the rhythm. That is, she circled every third number. 1 2 ③ 4 5 ⑥ 7 8 ⑨ 10 11 ⑫ 13 14 ⑮ 16 17 ⑱ 19 20 ㉑ 22 23 ㉔ 25 26 ㉗ 28 29 ㉚ 31 32 ㉝ 34 35 ㊱ Having finished this, she wiped the slate clean, leaving only the circled numbers.

    3   6   9   12 15 18 21 24 27 30 33 36

In the morning she had a new idea. Calling to Raymond she said," Raymond I'm going to make a slate of the threes as well. And I'm going to put the 'times' sign of Multiplicando and also use the 'equals' sign he showed us from the Golden Scale."

When she'd written up to 36 = 12 X 3 she couldn't bear the thought of erasing it, so she decided to ask her parents if she could have a second slate. She leaned it up, against the wall of her chamber, and, looking at it, wondered what Multiplicando had meant that day in the courtyard when he had said 'twos table'. Suddenly, she had an inkling, and she wrote:

Rosemary's Table of Threes

$$3 = 1 \times 3$$
$$6 = 2 \times 3$$
$$9 = 3 \times 3$$
$$12 = 4 \times 3$$
$$15 = 5 \times 3$$
$$18 = 6 \times 3$$
$$21 = 7 \times 3$$
$$24 = 8 \times 3$$
$$27 = 9 \times 3$$
$$30 = 10 \times 3$$
$$33 = 11 \times 3$$
$$36 = 12 \times 3$$

FOURS

The twins loved to visit their friend, Walter the Wheelwright, in his shop. Walter was a very careful worker, very proud of his work. Sometimes, when the twins peered in the door, they would hear him saying, "EVERY WHEEL MUST BE RIGHT TO BE A WALTER WHEELWRIGHT WHEEL." They didn't in any way want to offend him, but they found themselves whispering these words, just because they were such fun to say. They could see how he worked, always the same way. As he would finish the wheels for one wagon he would lay them out in two pairs, two wheels for the front, and two for the back.

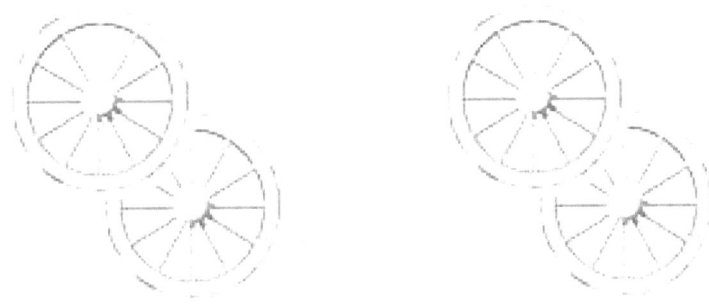

This day Rosemary didn't feel like staying to chat with Walter, but Raymond stayed behind. On her way home Rosemary decided to count her twos by two. This was a way of counting fours, she realized. She started a counting march, beginning with two, counting by two and stepping hard on the second number ... 2 **4** 6 **8** 10 **12** 14 **16** 18 **20** ... all the way home. On her slate she wrote this out and circled every second number. 2 (4) 6 (8) 10 (12) 14 (16) 18 (20) 22 (24) 26 (28) 30 (32) 34 (36) 38 (40) 42 (44) 46 (48)...

Then she wiped the slate clean, and wrote out her fours:

      4   8   12   16   20   24   28   32   36   40   44   48

That evening she took out her new slate and wrote:

Rosemary's Table of Fours

4	= 1 × 4	28	= 7 × 4
8	= 2 × 4	32	= 8 × 4
12	= 3 × 4	36	= 9 × 4
16	= 4 × 4	40	= 10 × 4
20	= 5 × 4	44	= 11 × 4
24	= 6 × 4	48	= 12 × 4

Rosemary couldn't wait to show Multiplicando what she had accomplished, both the slate of fours, and her 'table' of fours.

"You've done well, Rosemary," he said with a twinkle in his eyes. "And you guessed right to use the 'equals' sign, and the 'times' sign AND the title *Table of Fours*!" Just like that he did 12 cartwheels to show his appreciation. She couldn't help counting as he did each one. "*4 8 12 16 20 24 28 32 36 40 44 48*." When they had finished counting the fours, Multiplicando stood there spread-eagled with his head thrown back. Rosemary could have had no bigger reward.

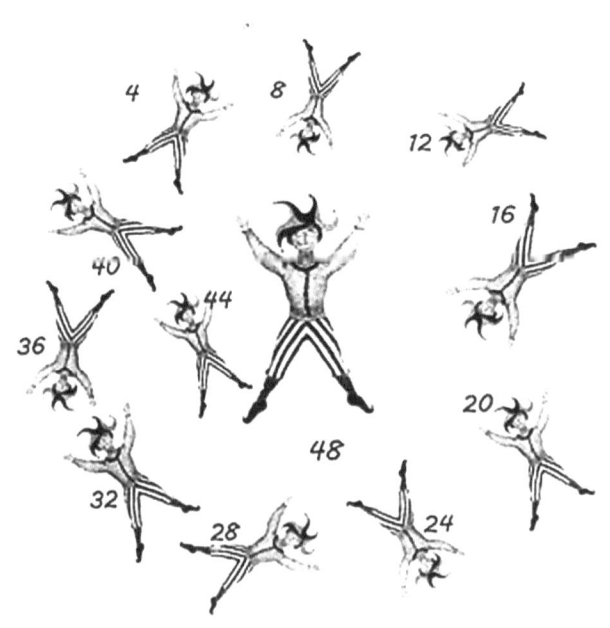

THE SIGN OF KING DIVIDE

One day the twins ran into Multiplicando atop the castle tower, where he had been practicing juggling. Now Raymond stepped forward to ask a question that he'd been burning to ask ever since Multiplicando had arrived. "Multiplicando, when are you going to tell us why you call our father 'King Divide'?"

"And our mother, 'Her Highness Minus'," added Rosemary.

"Well, I suppose there's no time like the present," answered Multiplicando. "Did you know that your father actually came from very humble beginnings? He was living with his mother, tending sheep, in a tiny cottage on the outermost reaches of the kingdom. This was in the time of the Great Famine, which many people still remember. Food was very scarce, and people were dying of hunger. The reason for this was that the old king had quarreled with an evil magician who, in revenge, had put the kingdom under a spell. This he had done by turning a loaf of bread into a stone. Until someone could split this stone, nothing would grow in the kingdom. The water dried up, and with it the crops. The king sent messengers to all corners of the kingdom to find young men worthy of the task. The one who succeeded would receive half the kingdom and the hand in marriage of Princess Hellene." Raymond and Rosemary looked at each other sheepishly.

Multiplicando continued, "Now, the square all roundabout the stone lay strewn with broken swords. Worse, the kingdom's storehouses were nearly empty. All the messengers had returned, save one, Roderick. Truth to tell, dear Roderick, had gotten lost. In wandering through the highlands he found himself in need of shelter, and noticing smoke coming from a tidy little cottage, he knocked at the door. He was greeted by a red-haired lad little more than a boy, who said, 'Please come in, and be welcome. There is a warm place for you by the hearth. My name is David, and this is my mother'.

"'What brings you to this out of the way place?' the woman inquired in a kind voice. So Roderick related the entire story, nearly leaving off the challenge, for the boy was so young. But when he heard the challenge, David swelled with courage, and within seconds, had made up his mind to go. Over the hearth hung an old sword, which his dear grandfather had once used in battle. Taking it down, he prepared to leave first thing in the morning. Bidding his mother good-bye, he and Roderick, set off for the palace."

Multiplicando continued. "Withered crops and starving cattle met them everywhere, but that was nothing compared to the desperate looks in the eyes of the people they encountered. At long last they arrived in the royal city. David looked around the square and, indeed, it was much as Roderick had described. Undaunted, he uttered a silent prayer, and summoning all his strength he raised his grandfather's sword overhead. Then, thinking of his dear grandfather, with all his heart and with all his might, he brought the sword down right in the center of the stone. Miraculously the stone split in two. Roderick was amazed.

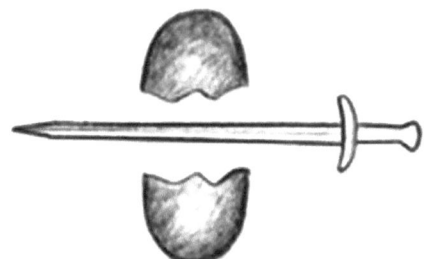

"The rest of the folk had not even bothered to watch. Yet, flowers blossomed and birds sang. Before long, people did begin to realize what had happened. Word was sent to the king. At length, he appeared with his daughter, Princess Hellene, at his side. The king embraced David. The young princess' eyes met David's eyes." Raymond and Rosemary blushed once again to think of their mother as a young princess and of their father as a mere lad.

"A grand wedding was celebrated, and David's mother was brought to the palace to live," Multiplicando went on. "After a number of years, the old king died, and your father became king, your mother queen. Sometime after that, you two came into the world."

The two looked at each other once again. "But, Multiplicando," asked Raymond insistently, "how did my father come to be called 'King Divide'?"

"Yes, of course, I almost forgot your original question, didn't I? Well, you see, after the great deed of cleaving the stone was accomplished, the old king declared that every loaf of bread baked in the kingdom was to bear the imprint of this sign."

"Yes, I see. Here is the sword, and on either side are the pieces of the bread," said Raymond.

"And, and," said Rosemary, "that stands for dividing?"

"Correcto!" said Multiplicando. "But, dear children, there is more to the story that I want Roderick himself to tell. Go seek him out."

The children were off in a flash to seek out Roderick, who was now the king's chief steward.

WHAT RODERICK TOLD THEM

"Roderick," said Raymond, "Multiplicando says that you can tell us why our father is called 'King Divide'. Not about the sword business, something else."

"Ah, yes, I know what you mean. Well, I'm sure you remember the part of the story where I came upon your father's little cottage. There was something particular that I sensed right away, but it wasn't until the next morning that I realized just what it was. The cottage and the grounds around it were particularly neat and orderly, just like the kingdom is today. For one thing, outside the cottage the firewood was neatly stacked. The largest and heaviest of the logs were stacked with 2 on the bottom and 1 on the top, 3 in all. Middle-sized logs had 3 on the bottom, then 2 and then 1 on the top, 6 in all. Then there were the thinnest logs stacked 4, 3, 2, 1 ..."

 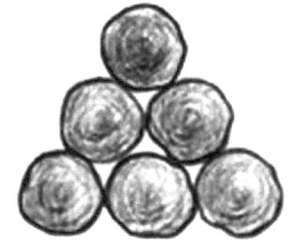 

"Ten in all," blurted out Raymond, who was just waiting for the opportunity.

"Good for you my boy," responded Roderick. "But that was not all there was," he went on. "I also remember that there were sheep pens, three of them, each with the same number of sheep. Your father kept them that way. On the way back, he confided in me that he was never quite comfortable when there was not an even number of sheep in them. It was the same with the rabbit hutches. The quicker the rabbits multiplied, the faster he divided them up. He's still that way with everything."

"Now," said Raymond, "I can certainly see why he is called 'King Divide'.

WHICH THINGS COME IN WHATS

"It was so interesting to hear Roderick speak of when Father was a boy, wasn't it, Rose."

"Yes, it certainly was," she agreed.

"Well, I was thinking that some things want to be divided up in a certain way just because of what they are," said Raymond.

"Like the way the heaviest logs were in threes because they would have been too heavy to lift any higher," responded Rosemary.

"Yes, exactly," said Raymond. "Let's see which things come in whats, okay."

"Sure," said Rosemary, "I can think of something right off, shoes and gloves. They both come in pairs because we have two hands and two feet."

"Everything that comes in pairs is two, said Raymond." "Yes," replied Rosemary. "Now, how about threes?" "Milking stools!" blurted out Raymond.

"That's right, Raymond. Do you remember the time John the Joiner made milking stools for all the milkmaids at once, how he carefully laid out the legs, three by three? I think he made nine stools altogether. How many legs was that?"

Raymond wasn't sure he was ready for this. How much was 9 times 3 anyway? Then he remembered that 10 times 3 is 30, so he just took three away. "27?" he said, questioningly.

"Why, Raymond, that was quite impressive," his sister said. "How about fours?"

"Well of course, there are Walter's wheels, four wheels for every wagon," answered Rosemary, "but so many things come in fours. Think of it, everything square has four sides. Chairs and tables have four legs, and their tops have four sides, too."

Raymond shut his eyes,

> Rooms have four walls
> Big or small,
> Even the chicken coop
> And the horses' stalls.

"Not bad, Raymond," said Rosemary. "You made that rhyme very nicely. How about fives? Fingers," she called, answering her own question.

"Not fair," claimed Raymond.

"You're right, it wasn't fair, but listen, we both know that fingers and toes come in fives, and even in tens. That's not the hard part. What I want to know is what comes in sixes, sevens eights and nines?"

"It could be like the sheep pens," exclaimed Raymond.

"Raymond, I think you're on to something. Sometimes things are grouped into sixes and sometimes the same things are grouped into sevens, depending on how many there are. Just like with Father's sheep pens."

"Or how many plants are planted in a bed, or arrows in an archer's quiver for that matter. Or how many stones to each catapult," added Raymond.

SHARE FAIR AND SQUARE

In the afternoon, Raymond was playing with his best friends, Hugh and Guy. They had been granted permission to pick the last of the plums. "Remember," said Hugh, "we share fair and square."

"Oh, yes," they all chorused, "we share fair and square."

There were 12 plums left on the tree, and these were quickly picked by the hungry boys. "Now," said Raymond, "let's share them out." So one by one, each in turn took a plum from the pile.

"Hold it," said Raymond suddenly, "we don't need to count them out, we each get four. Twelve is three fours."

Well, of course they did need to count them out just to see if Raymond was right. "You were right!" shouted Guy, in the end.

Just at that moment, their friend Roger appeared, and the boys knew that what held for three held for four. "Let's each give Roger one of ours to start with," said Hugh.

"To start with, to finish with," said Raymond. "Four threes make twelve, too. Three for each of us."

"We share fair and square," the boys chorused.

That evening, Raymond got out his pouch of favorite rocks. Then he took 12 sticks and made three sheep pens. Counting out 18 rocks, he divided them equally among the pens. Here are my sheep, six sheep in each," he announced. "Just as I had guessed."

Next he took out 27, again dividing them equally among the pens. "Nine in each," he counted to himself. "Just as I thought."

HER HIGHNESS MINUS

Next time the twins caught up, Multiplicando was practicing juggling in the Great Hall. "Multiplicando," Rosemary blurted out, "you have never explained to us why you call Mother 'Her Highness Minus'."

"Why that's right!" acknowledged Multiplicando, slowing down from 6 balls to 5 to 4 to 3 to 2 to one, which he just tossed up and down until he stopped altogether. "I most certainly have not. Well, as they say, there's no time like the present."

"Your dear mother, as you well know, is counted among the most generous of women. She had taken it upon herself to distribute bread to the poor of the kingdom. When folk came to her, she would see to it that they got their fair share. The king saw to it that Reginald the Record Keeper was always there. One time I drew a sketch of the queen and showed it to Reginald. He noticed the open-handed way she gave away bread.

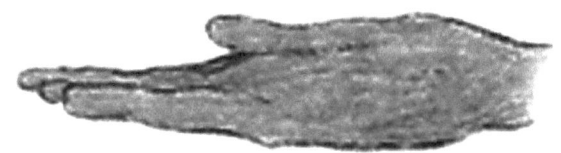

Now, like a good mathematician, he uses the short form of her hand to record 'giving away.' An example of what he wrote would be

$$8 - 2 = 6$$

Well of course you know that giving away is the opposite of 'adding to.' Giving away, or taking away for that matter, leaves less than before. 'Minus' is a word which means 'less', thus I came to call your mother 'Her Highness Minus', and it's been like that ever since. Of course your mother put things another way altogether. She said that when we give away we may have less, but we also have more, more joy in giving!"

GIVING AWAY IN A FAST WAY

"Now," Multiplicando went on, "there were problems, but problems can bring forth new ideas. Of course lines could get very long when bread was given out, especially when food was scarce. People might wait for hours, and then get to the bread pantry and find no bread was left. The king and queen agreed that this must not happen again. Here's how they solved the problem."

"People, it seems, took away 3 loaves at a time, a good ration. Usually, Reginald would keep a running tally, always taking away 3 more. You know,

18 − 3 = 15   *15 − 3 = 12*   *12 − 3 = 9*   *9 − 3 = 6*   *6 − 3 = 3*

It works, but it's slow. And it doesn't help the people at the end of the line. One day as I watched at the door of the pantry, I felt I needed to sketch the bread inside the pantry. There it was like this: Inside the pantry were the loaves Gus had baked. Now that could be a big number. So, just to keep it simple, let's say there are 30 loaves. Three was the number of loaves each took away. What wasn't known was..."

"... how many people could be served?" blurted out Raymond.

"Correcto," said Multiplicando. "So, how many people could be served?"

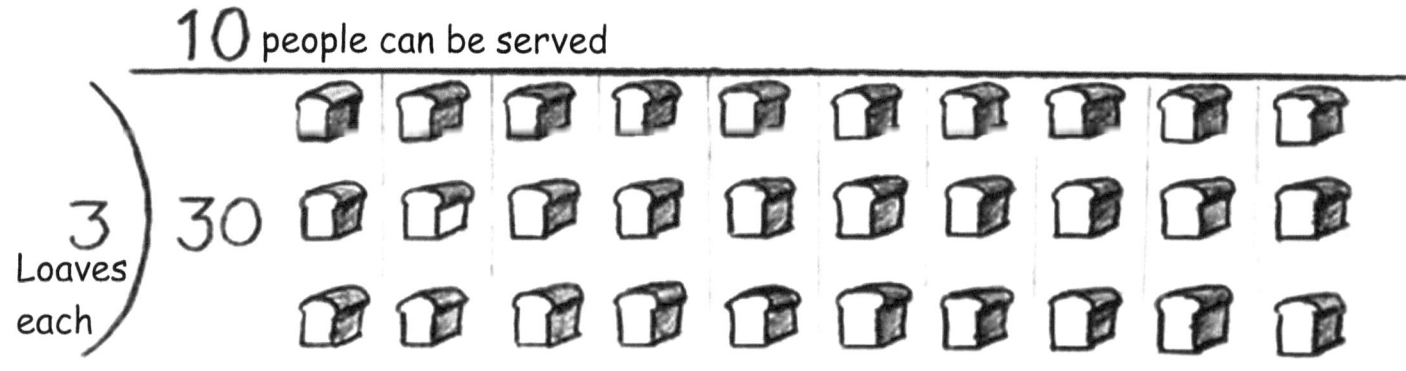

Total number of loaves in the pantry

"Ten," shouted Raymond triumphantly. He didn't know how or why he knew, but he knew.

"Correcto!" cried Multiplicando.

"So that's how it's done," cried out Rosemary. "Now I see. And then the rest of the people can come back the next day and not have to waste their time waiting in line."

"Correcto!"

CHECKING

That night Rosemary had a hard time getting to sleep. Taking up her candle she got up to look at her 3's slate. She said all the number facts to herself and then got back in bed. Then a rhyme started to form in her mind. Starting part way through, she began.

4	3	12	4 x 3 is 12	12 ÷ 3 is 4
5	3	15	5 x 3 is 15	15 ÷ 3 is 5
6	3	18	6 x 3 is 18	18 ÷ 3 is 6

The next morning when Raymond awoke, he saw the sun shining directly onto Rosemary's tablet of 3's. Now it was his turn to make a discovery. In all the excitement he had never had a chance to try out his numbers from the sheep pens. Now he saw the number facts neatly written out—*21 24 27*—those were the numbers they were working with. How many times can *21* sheep be separated into 3 pens? There it was, clear as day, right on the line, *7*. He clapped his hands with joy. "Now what about *24* sheep," he wondered out loud. There it is, *8* times.

Now what about **27** sheep? Simple, *9* times *3*.

Rosemary, who had awoken from all the excitement, said, "Yes it's right there on the tablet. Now all we need to do is memorize what's on the tables, learn them by heart."

"That won't be hard," said Raymond, not the way I feel."

The twins had to find Multiplicando to tell him of their discovery. He was speaking with the king in the Great Hall when they found him. They shared everything they had discovered, and both the king and Multiplicando were very pleased.

"So," said the king, "now you can see, perhaps, why Multiplicando and I have always felt like brothers."

"How so, Father?" asked Raymond.

"Well you see, multiplying and dividing are really just the exact opposite of each other. That is why when we divide, we check to make sure we're right by saying.

3 goes into 15   5 times   because 5 X 3 is 15
or
3 goes into 30   10 times   because 10 X 3 is 30

"I think I almost understand," said Raymond. Everyone laughed.

DOUBLE THREEs

"Hey, Rose, remember how you counted by 2s to get your 4s. Well, I tried it with 6s. I just counted by 3, stamping on the second one, *3 **6** 9 **12** 15 **18** 21 **24** 27 **30** 33 **36**.* Once I passed *36* it was a little harder, but I just did Multiplicando's special step, step, leap when I needed to."

Rosemary decided to write this out on another slate. She was enjoying lining up all the tables along the wall of her chamber, and very glad her parents had given her as many slates as she needed. First she circled every other 3. As she did, Raymond noticed something.

"Look, Rose," he said excitedly, "the second of the pair is always even."

"Well, what do you know," she said, quite amazed. "But then again, it shouldn't be surprising." Rosemary held up three fingers on one hand. "Look," she said, "when I hold up three fingers on the other hand and put them together, they look very even."

"You're right," said Raymond. "Steven would like that."

Rosemary's Table of Sixes

$6 = 1 \times 6$
$12 = 2 \times 6$
$18 = 3 \times 6$
$24 = 4 \times 6$
$30 = 5 \times 6$
$36 = 6 \times 6$

$42 = 7 \times 6$
$48 = 8 \times 6$
$54 = 9 \times 6$
$60 = 10 \times 6$
$66 = 11 \times 6$
$72 = 12 \times 6$

DOUBLE FOURS AND TRIPLE THREEs

"If it works by doubling three to make six, do you suppose we can get to eight by doubling four?" suggested Rosemary.

"I bet so," said Raymond. "Let's step it." So, together they marched.

4   *8*   12   *16*   20   *24*   28   *32*   36   *40*   44   *48* ...

Somewhere after *48* they lost count.

"Wow, that was hard," said Rosemary.

"Yeah," agreed Raymond. "Let's look on your Fours Table and see what happened."

"I see," said Rosemary. "I see the pattern.

$$2 \times 4 \quad is \quad 1 \times 8$$
$$4 \times 4 \quad is \quad 2 \times 8$$
$$6 \times 4 \quad is \quad 3 \times 8$$

So the 8s table is ...

```
8  is 1×8
16 is 2×8
24 is 3×8
32 is 4×8
40 is 5×8
48 is 6×8
```

"48 is where the 4s Table ended, isn't it," said Raymond. "We're only half way there, to 12 times. How are we going to get to 12X8," he asked, slightly worried.

"Don't worry," said Rosemary comfortingly.

"That's easy to say," said Raymond, "but I don't add so well with 8." "Raymond, I discovered that it's like adding 10 and giving 2 away. Like this:

8+10 is 18. Give away 2 makes 16.

16+10 is 26. Give away 2 makes 24."

"I almost get what you're saying," said Raymond, smiling. He was gazing at the slate. And, he had noticed something—another pattern!

"Look, Rose," he said, "the numbers on the right keep dropping down by two, while the ones on the left keep growing by one."

"You are right, brother. Look at that!"

Together they finished the 8s Table watching Raymond's pattern emerge before their eyes.

Rosemary's Table of Eights

8 is 1×8	56 is 7×8
16 is 2×8	64 is 8×8
24 is 3×8	72 is 9×8
32 is 4×8	80 is 10×8
40 is 5×8	88 is 11×8
48 is 6×8	96 is 12×8

The twins couldn't wait to see Multiplicando and to share their discoveries.

Now Rosemary was very interested in the pattern that Raymond had discovered. "What about 9?" she pondered as she lay in bed in the dark.

"9 is three 3s. 3, 6, 9." Just having said that, the rhythm clicked in:

*3   6   **9,**   12   15   **18,**   21   24   **27,**   30   33   **36***

She stopped. The echo of what she'd just said, 9 18 27 36 stood out in her mind, just as if she'd circled them. She could hear something familiar, a pattern, but she wasn't quite sure yet what it was. Rosemary recited as she wrote on a new slate:

9   18   27   36   45   54   63   72   81   90   ...

That's *10×9*. *90* and *9* is *99*, and then ... *108*. I can't wait for morning to come, so I can write out the 9s table."

The sun was shining in through the window as she finished. "Raymond, come see," she said.

Rosemary's Table of Nines

$9 = 1 \times 9$ $\qquad$ $63 = 7 \times 9$
$18 = 2 \times 9$ $\qquad$ $72 = 8 \times 9$
$27 = 3 \times 9$ $\qquad$ $81 = 9 \times 9$
$36 = 4 \times 9$ $\qquad$ $90 = 10 \times 9$
$45 = 5 \times 9$ $\qquad$ $99 = 11 \times 9$
$54 = 6 \times 9$ $\qquad$ $108 = 12 \times 9$

"Everything lines up so beautifully," he said.

"Yes, doesn't it," she agreed. Then she paused and whispered, "Now I see what I was hearing in the counting rhythm.

9
18
27
36
45
54
63
72
81
90
99
108

"I get it," Raymond said, knowingly.
"I really see. There's that up and down thing again.

WAYS OF SAYING

"Rosemary, what was the word that Father used before. Did he say 'multiplying'? He said it was the opposite of dividing."

"Yes, I think so. Multiplying is the thing we do when we act like Multiplicando, doing cartwheels over and over. 'Multiply' also means 'times', how many time you increase the number."

"You're right," said Raymond. "It's the same with 'dividing' isn't it? It's also called 'sharing fairly'..."

"Or grouping things in equal measure," added Rosemary. "With 2s, it is pairing up," said Raymond.

"Think of how many words there are for 'plus'," said Rosemary.

"Sure, there's 'adding to, increasing, getting more, gathering,' and on and on."

"Do you know what Reginald called 'giving away'?" said Rosemary. "He called it 'subtracting'. He said that's the word that real mathematicians use."

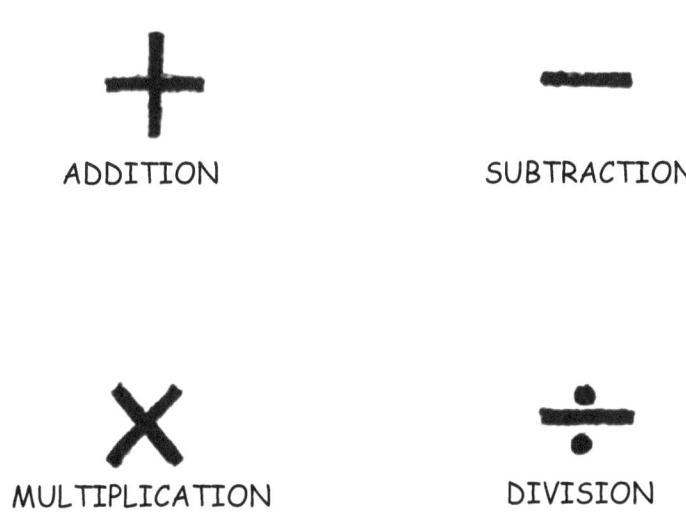

ROSEMARY DREAMS ELEVEN

Rosemary loved to accompany her mother to the garden, where they would cut tulips and roses and other flowers to be given away. The queen would arrange them, 10 to a vase, a good counting number.

One night, Rosemary lay in bed thinking about 11. She found herself picturing it as one full vase of 10 flowers, plus one flower on the table beside it. Soon afterward, she fell asleep. In her sleep, she saw vases lining up, one behind the other, with an extra flower beside each vase. As she looked down the table, she counted:

"10 and 1, 20 and 2, 30 and 3, 40 and 4..." When she awoke, she could still see the table with the vases. She took out a new tablet and started to write:

$$10 + 1 = 11$$
$$20 + 2 = 22$$
$$30 + 3 = 33$$
$$40 + 4 = 44$$
$$50 + 5 = 55$$
$$60 + 6 = 66$$
$$70 + 7 = 77$$

Raymond woke up when he heard the chalk on the slate. After he had shaken the cobwebs out of his head, he could see what his sister was doing.

"Let's see," he said, "in one column it goes:

$$10, 20, 30, 40, 50, 60, 70, 80, 90 \ldots$$

… and in another *1, 2, 3, 4, 5, 6, 7, 8, …*"

$$10 + 1 = 11$$
$$20 + 2 = 22$$
$$30 + 3 = 33$$
$$40 + 4 = 44$$
$$50 + 5 = 55$$
$$60 + 6 = 66$$
$$70 + 7 = 77$$
$$80 + 8 = 88$$
$$90 + 9 = 99$$

"… and in the last it goes *11, 22, 33, 44, 55, 66, 77, 88, 99.*"

SAME WITH TWELVES
A LITTLE DIFFERENT

About a week later, Rosemary once again dreamed of roses. The only difference this time was that instead of there being one rose on the table beside each vase, there were two.

When Raymond awoke, he could see what his sister was doing.

"Let's see," he said, "on one side it goes 10, 20, 30, 40... and, on the other, 2, 4, 6, 8... That's 10 and 2, 20 and 4, 30 and 6, 40 and 8, 50 and 10, which is SIXTY ... Alright, then it's ten more plus two. That's 72, 84, 96, 100 and, uh, 8..." "Keep going, Raymond," his sister urged.

"Alright, let's see, ten more is 118 plus 2 equals 120, 132 and 144. Done." Rosemary, of course, wrote out the 12s table like this:

Rosemary's Table of Twelves

$12 = 1 \times 12$	$84 = 7 \times 12$
$24 = 2 \times 12$	$96 = 8 \times 12$
$36 = 3 \times 12$	$108 = 9 \times 12$
$48 = 4 \times 12$	$120 = 10 \times 12$
$60 = 5 \times 12$	$132 = 11 \times 12$
$72 = 6 \times 12$	$144 = 12 \times 12$

MULTIPLICANDO'S TABLE

Raymond and Rosemary found more and more patterns hidden in the times tables. Currently, Rosemary was fascinated by the 9s. She loved the way the two columns went opposite directions, but she had an inkling of something else. She just didn't quite know what it was.

One day, she climbed the stairs to the battlements, taking the slate with the 9s Table on it with her. Raymond was already there, balancing on the parapets while watching the guards marching. Rosemary stared at the slate, and the numbers neatly lined up. Suddenly, she cried out, "I've got it! Raymond look at this. Do you see?"

"Yes. I see *1X9 = 9, 2X9 = 18, 3X9 = 27* and ..."

"No, no, not that," she interrupted. "It's much more magical. If you add 1 and 8 of 18, the 2 and 7 of 27, the 3 and 6 of 36, the 4 and 5 of 45, it always equals 9."

"Now I've seen everything!" shouted Raymond.

"Everything? Not quite." The twins looked up to see Multiplicando standing behind them. "You two must be magicians to have discovered all of these things, even the magic of nines."

"We're not magicians, but we are becoming mathematicians, aren't we," said Rosemary proudly.

"You certainly are," said Multiplicando. "And before I leave…" "Leave?" said Raymond, crestfallen.

"Yes, my friends, I must be going from here to there, but before I do, I wanted to show you something. Come."

This time, Multiplicando could hardly keep up with Raymond and Rosemary as the twins sprinted ahead of him up the twisting tower stairs. As they entered the sun-washed room, Rosemary sighed deeply and said, "I feel so new inside, so new with knowledge."

"Yes," said Multiplicando, "you really are."

Raymond, meanwhile, had wandered over to the table. What he saw, filled him with wonder. "Look," he said, touching the numbers inlaid with gold—

2 4 6 8...   3 6 9 12...   4 8 12 16...   5 10 15 20...   6 12 18 24
Rosemary joined him by the table. "Yes!" she exclaimed, excitedly.

"7 14 21 28...   8 16 24 32...   9 18 27 36...
10 20 30 40...   11 22 33 44...   12 24 36 48...
It's all here. All of the tables in one!"

"Yes, it is," said Multiplicando, "and once you've learned it, you will never, ever forget."

1	2	3	4	5	6	7	8	9	10	11	12
2	4	6	8	10	12	14	16	18	20	22	24
3	6	9	12	15	18	21	24	27	30	33	36
4	8	12	16	20	24	28	32	36	40	44	48
5	10	15	20	25	30	35	40	45	50	55	60
6	12	18	24	30	36	42	48	54	60	66	72
7	14	21	28	35	42	49	56	63	70	77	84
8	16	24	32	40	48	56	64	72	80	88	96
9	18	27	36	45	54	63	72	81	90	99	108
10	20	30	40	50	60	70	80	90	100	110	120
11	22	33	44	55	66	77	88	99	110	121	132
12	24	36	48	60	72	84	96	108	120	132	144

THE END

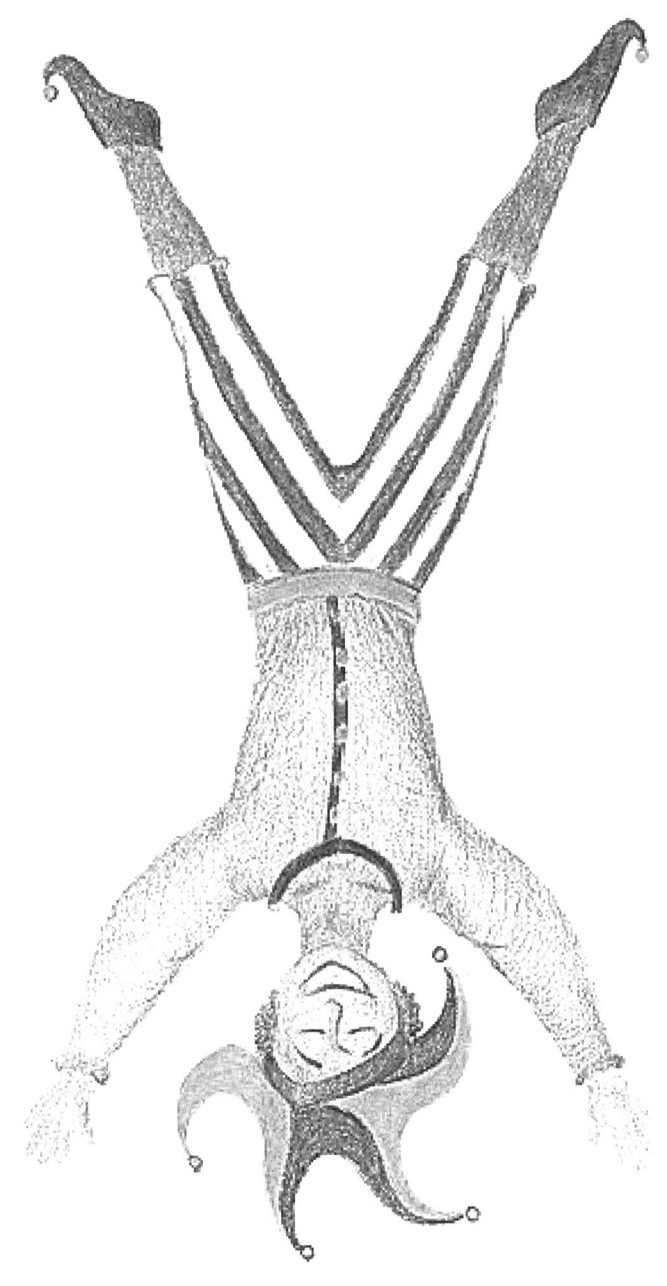

Using Multiplicando

A Manual

Using Multiplicando

Multiplicando is a teaching story. It seeks to present traditional "academic material" in story form. Its main focus is the process of multiplication, yet multiplication cannot rightly be presented without treatment of the related processes, addition, subtraction and division. As this connection is genuine, integral and real, children will feel a certain affirmation in this approach. It has been found that in this imaginative approach, multiplication is easily grasped by first grade students, and it is to this age level that *Multiplicando* is primarily directed, though children at nearly any age find it appealing. While this approach may seem like an extreme departure from traditional educational practices, and it is, the validity of this approach has been verified for nearly 100 years in Waldorf schools world-wide.

The story contains characters who themselves embark on a path of learning. Children may thereby develop a warmer feeling for this subject which may otherwise perhaps be experienced as distant and abstract. Even to those who take to math with ease, this imaginative approach can broaden the scope and extent of the experience into the kinesthetic and feeling realms through rhythmical movement and artistic activity. This approach works with the innate rhythmical and imaginative faculties of children in the early school years. It leads them through a series of experiences, and from this to a grasp of the inherent mathematical principles.

Learning With *Multiplicando* – The activities of the characters in the story of *Multiplicando* suggest activities. As Raymond and Rosemary work through their experiences with their teacher, Multiplicando, we can follow them on their path into the world of mathematics. The story of *Multiplicando* was written in such a way as to suggest pedagogical activities. This manual is an attempt to clarify and bring to light what may not be readily apparent.

Telling the Story of *Multiplicando* – As with any story book, *Multiplicando* may be read, or it may be told. To do either the story teller/teacher must, to a greater or lesser extent, know the story, own it. The story breaks down into manageable components, roughly corresponding with the chapters, which may be related over the course of days or weeks as proves convenient, or assimilable to the students. Of course "telling" a story may at first seem a daunting task. However, once one has become familiar with them, the scenes are relatively simple to relate. They must, however, become living within the teacher or parent.

Acting Out *Multiplicando* – Children enjoy acting out vignettes taken from *Multiplicando*. This type of work is well worth the time in the long run (and it needn't take long). Few activities work more profoundly on children, connecting them deeply with what they are learning. Simply, identify the characters, picture where they are standing, and assign dialog from the text.

Creating a Companion Book – You can follow the learning process undergone by Raymond and Rosemary, recording your experiences in pictures and symbols in a blank art book or sketch pad (8 ½ X 11 or larger). Doing this enables the student to participate artistically, and thus to take the story into his/her inner life of feeling and imagination. Times tables may be written on a chalkboard first and then entered in the companion book. Alternatively, freestanding pages may be drawn and glued to cardboard backing and leaned against the wall, as per the story.

Illustrations – Illustrations may be drawn to accompany any scene. They may be artistic or schematic. The more artistic they are the more the creative element enters into the mood of the learning. To combine seemingly diverse subjects may have a beneficial, synergistic effect.

Reinforcing Lessons Learned from Multiplicando – There is a strong element of rhythmicity in mathematics. Many of the activities connected with Multiplicando reflect this. Skipping, hopping, rhythmic counting, clapping, etc. occur naturally in children's wholesome play. In this way children get a leg up on learning. The spontaneous occurrence of this activity in childhood should help us realize that working with this "rhythmical faculty" in children is working with them, not going against their grain.

MULTIPLICANDO pp.1-2

This chapter sets the tone for the story to come. Multiplicando is a positive, enthusiastic figure, tripping lightly over the earth, yet grounded in knowledge. The STEP STEP LEAP, SHORT SHORT LONG, or anapest rhythm, is an outgoing, optimistic one, in the spirit of healthy childhood feeling. Multiplicando looks forward to his visit to the castle, and his friends, the king and queen.

The attempt is made here to connect math learning with the poetic, artistic element of the language arts. "There's the ma gi cian, math e ma ti cian" presages the revelations mathematics has to reveal, a storehouse of knowledge and interconnectedness. Each half of the phrase above has 5 beats. It is like a poetic, metrical equality. He might equally well have called himself a "mathemagician".

The stepping stones Multiplicando had laid out the last time he'd passed by were in the same SHORT SHORT LONG, rhythmically repeating pattern that he characteristically skipped in. In the THREES chapter they will reappear as 1 2 <u>3</u> 4 5 <u>6</u> 7 8 <u>9</u> 10 11 <u>12</u>. Like King Divide whom we encounter later, Multiplicando cannot help doing things in a rhythmical way.

Movement Activity: STEP STEP LEAP (to straddle position) while reciting Multiplicando's verse. A variation is to extend the arms outwards on the long beat, too.

Illustration Suggestions: Draw the castle, or Multiplicando skipping through the forest. Drawing CIRCLE – CIRCLE – OVAL, as in the illustration on p.2, is essential.

GUS PLUS pp. 3-4

We are moving from simple adding to fast, rhythmical adding, or multiplication. Yet this is a good opportunity to review adding, while demonstrating how multiplying is preferred in many situations.

Adding Activity: Use manipulatives, even real cookies, and place them randomly. You might notice geometrical forms such as triangles, squares or hexagons which spontaneously arise in the seeming randomness. Now do this on paper. Circle groupings and label them. Teach adding through finding convenient combinations, such as numbers totaling 10. Yet, encourage confidence that any addends may be combined equally well with practice.

After having practiced this way, move on to Multiplicando's way of counting. Of course, laying the objects out "like the five-card in the king's deck", means 2 above, 2 below and 1 in the middle.

Regrouping Activity: Regroup the cookies, etc. into fives as in the illustration. Then count the ones in the middle, which gives you how many 5s there are. Count by 5 that number of times, in this case 4 times. Over time this will become almost automatic.

Illustration: Draw the comparative picture as shown in the illustrations. Label BEFORE MULTIPLICANDO and AFTER MULTIPLICANDO, GUS' WAY and MULTIPLICANDO'S WAY, or whatever you choose. This may be schematic, or include characters, cookies, oven, etc.

Counting by fives seems to come naturally to children because of its unique rhythmicity. They learn it by heart as they would a rhyme. You can imitate Multiplicando by standing spread-eagled and feigning a cartwheel each time a 5 is counted.

Write out 5 10 15 20 25 30 35 40 45 50 55 60, or variously 5 ^{10} 15 ^{20} 25 ^{30} and so on... to give a picture of the alternation of five and zero. Lay a rope on the floor and jump back and forth counting 5s on one side and 10s on the other, feet together.

Although Multiplicando introduces the (phrase) 4 *times* 5 is 20, there is no need to explain this concept at this time. Just let it sink in as far as it goes for now. It will be repeated many times in the course of the story.

THE TOWER ROOM (pp.5-7)

The scene of Raymond and Rosemary whispering to each other is a favorite of the children. It is fun to act it out with the 5 characters, the king, the queen, Multiplicando, Raymond and Rosemary. Unless you have a simple weighing scale you have to be creative with this. Your hands held in front of you at waist level actually work quite well to simulate a scale. Express the inequalities by holding one hand lower than the other. However, since the knowledge we are primarily seeking to develop is an abstract mathematical one, we would do equally well with two circles representing the pans. Add or subtract numbers until the trays balance. Record the equations on paper. This is better done the following day as a review.

Illustration- Draw the Golden Scale and then highlight a section of the cross beam. On the side, or below, neatly draw the equals sign. Tip: A dotted line will produce a more satisfying chain than a solid one. The pans should be slightly oval-shaped.

TODD AND STEVEN (pp.8-9)

This amusing activity helps create a visual basis for various forms of counting in a way similar to what adding two dice does in board games. It makes visible what some people do unconsciously and may aid those children who otherwise may have trouble adding.

The scenario may be acted out at a long, rectangular table (several desks put together). It could also be done using counters and imaginary people placed on rectangular 'tables'. Choose up to 12 patrons of the inn who then decide among themselves how many will be seated at first (assign a spokesman, or leader). When the second group is being seated Todd and Steven wrangle over who is to wait on them (this is perhaps best mimed). As they are seated they follow the rule of the land by sitting opposite the odd one, if there is one.

Illustration – After having acted this out, you may draw a full-scale illustration of the table with food and drink, or simply a long rectangle with circles representing the goblets or mugs. Elsewhere you could draw say 3 dots and then 5 next to that. The open space across from the third, or odd dot, would then be filled by the odd dot of the 5. Orient the two quantities when they are separate so that the odd one of the 5 can slide right into the vacant slot. Somehow this feels like a preparation for work with valences in chemistry.

When Rosemary says, "It's definitely easier to count the evens," and Raymond replies, "But not that much harder with the odds," it is an attempt to acknowledge that children while learning undergo a process which can engender feelings of doubt or failure, and they are somehow comforted to know that other children also have to grapple in a similar way. Further, they may come to see that the process of learning is interesting, in and of itself.

TWOS (pp.10-11)

Here we begin formally with the times tables. The students keep the rhythm just as Raymond and Rosemary do, first clapping and then stamping or marching. Thus, they count to 24, first saying the odd numbers softly and then omitting them altogether. Ultimately, they are counting by 2s. This "every other" rhythm is fundamental to times table work. A like rhythm in verse, the iamb, could go: I keep the beat with hands or feet; or "Be strong, be bold, your heart's of gold; I meet the need, I do the deed..." Write out the numbers 1-24, then underline the even numbers. Multiplicando's cartwheels represent the number of times 2 to is added to itself.

A fundamental movement activity – Say 2 is 1x2, 4 is 2x2 accompanying each word with the following series of movements: CLAP – CLAP – HOP – CROSS – HOP. The HOP is a leap to a straddle or spread position, the CROSS is a crossing of the legs. The word straddle could be substituted for hop.

Variations: There are many variations of this rhythm. This activity may accompany the learning of each of the times tables. Rhythm sticks may be used to keep the beat, or bean bags may be tossed rhythmically.

THAT NIGHT (p.12)

Raymond and Rosemary practice the rudiments of multiplying. Raymond utilizes the experience with Todd and Steven to find the correct answers. Practice following the example of Raymond and Rosemary, perhaps trying to visualize the table at Todd and Steven's Inn. It doesn't matter if the facts are all correct at first. The next chapter will further reinforce the students' facility with the process. The ultimate goal is to know the multiplication facts out of order.

Illustration: Be sure to draw the picture of Multiplicando as Raymond did. The picture can be as simple or as detailed as you wish. Multiplicando may be given a different costume or physiognomy. Be aware that the X shape should clearly underlie the picture. A light-colored sketch, in yellow perhaps, may be attempted first for practice and then be drawn over.

THE SIGN OF MULTIPLICANDO (p.13)

The 2s table, like the others that follow, shows graphically the rhythmical nature of multiplication. The product increases by 2 while the multiplier increases by 1. Keeping the columns lined up is important. It is a good idea to skip a space between each multiplication fact to keep them from running together. Perhaps begin by listing the 2s vertically at the left of the page. Having completed that, then write is 1X2 and so on. You can list all twelve facts in one column or split the page in half. You may also write out each number fact from beginning to end, for eg., 2 is 1X2. Give children time to discover the patterns revealed in the table. The product increases by 2, the multiplier increases by 1, and the multiplicand (2) stays the same. This may be done on an actual slate, writing with chalk.

If you are replicating Rosemary's slate in a companion book and want to keep the slate motif in mind, color in background afterward with dark blue or purple. Otherwise use a variety of colors to write with. Use them to bring out the fact that the multiplicand, 2, remains the same, while the multiplier increases by one. The times sign is best kept a consistent color. Children must pay careful attention if they are to do a neat job.

THREES (pp.14-15)

The anapest rhythm reappears. Here is an opportunity to integrate arts and math. Step or clap the rhythm while speaking Rosemary's poem. Add to it. Recall Multiplicando's verse at the outset of the story. Try creating original rhymes in the short, short, long meter. Perhaps there is a subject you want to treat, a situation to describe, a feeling you want to express. If not, just stepping the rhythm could elicit one. A well- known verse goes:

> Brave and true/Will I be/Each good deed/Sets me free/Each kind word/Makes me strong/
> I will fight/For the right/I will con/quer the wrong.

Count each step 1-36 with the third step being a straddle jump. Recall Multiplicando's stepping stones.

Face a partner and then cross clap right on 1/Cross clap left on 2/Clap both hands of partner on 3, and so on till 36.

Bean bag from Rt to Left hand on 1/Left to Rt on 2/Toss up and catch on 3.

Write out the 3s, (3 6 9 12 15 18 21 24 27 30 33 36). You may derive this by first writing the numbers 1- 36 and then underlining every third one. Do it on practice paper or a slate once and then in the companion book. Like Rosemary, write out the Table of Threes.

FOURS (pp.16-17)

Children enjoy acting out the opening scene. Walter proudly states EVERY WHEEL MUST BE RIGHT TO BE A WALTER WHEELWRIGT WHEEL. (Perhaps the class can first do it as a tongue twister.) Meanwhile, while he's facing the other way, Raymond and Rosemary peer in the doorway and whisper to each other.

Layout the wheels (pennies may be used) in sets of 2 pairs, skip counting them 2 4, 6 8, 10 12...

Find other things that come in 4s. A furniture maker would assemble 4 legs for each table or chair, for example. Match sticks or toothpicks would provide good manipulatives.

Write out the numbers 1-48, drawing a circle, or a square, around every 4th one. Then write out the 4s (4 8 12 16 20 24 28 32 36 40 44 48) as you did with the 3s.

Finally, replicate Rosemary's Table of Fours.

The 48 Club: Fours present a wonderful opportunity to introduce a strengthening activity. I call it The 48 Club. To do it the children count in unison while stepping onto a chair, and then back down again clapping on the 4s. Thus, step up on 1, with the second foot on 2, step down with one foot on 3, step down with other and clap on 4, and so on to 48. Once a rhythm is established after a number of days, or weeks, omit saying all but the 4s. This may also be done on a step, a low wall, a stump, etc. When a child can accomplish this on their own they become a member of the 48 Club. They may receive a stamp, a certificate, or have their name added to a list. This need not exclude anyone. If stepping up onto a chair is too difficult a lower object may be substituted.

THE SIGN OF KING DIVIDE (pp.18-20)

It would be good to begin learning this story some weeks prior to telling it. Remember, it need not be told word for word. The story lends an imaginative context for a symbol which otherwise is abstract. The human element "warms" the abstraction.

Illustration: Merely drawing the symbol on page 18 will suffice to link the symbol with the division process. However, children enjoy first drawing the plaza with the stone in the center and bits of broken swords lying about. Determine which picture is more compelling to draw, the desolate before scene (even as the sword is brought down) or the picture with the split stone and flowers already beginning to bloom.

WHAT RODERICK TOLD THEM (p.21)

This chapter further develops the description of the division process, the separation into groups. There is room for a lot of manipulatives work within this chapter. Dowels of 3 different diameters could be stacked to represent the logs. Pretzels, rolls of coins, or even real firewood logs could serve equally well. Pennies or discs of some kind could represent them in two dimensions. Note that the stacks form triangles. The Greeks referred to 3, 6, and 10 as triangular numbers.

WHICH THINGS COME IN WHATS (pp.22-23)

This chapter attempts to connect the mathematical process of division with situations in the real world. The scene involving the boys can easily be acted out using real fruit, or a replacement. Dialog may be created. It will be easy to find other situations from your own and the children's experience. We are experiencing that there is a natural tendency to group things equally and rhythmically. Rosemary begins to apply the times tables to the process of division. It is as if she is experiencing the echo of the multiplication rhythms.

SHARE FAIR AND SQUARE (pp.24-25)

Division is approached from a social context of fairness and sharing. We also take a step back to simpler problems. 12 is a fine number to divide as it can be divided by 1, 2, 3, 4, 6 and 12. Try dividing 12 students up, using the previously mentioned numbers as divisors. Try having them stand in 3 lines of 4, as if in a parade, or 4 lines of 3. Here we see that 4 threes is different than 3 fours. The product is the same, but the situation described is different. I call it "same answer, different story". The story of the fourth friend's arrival reinforces this.

It is useful to demonstrate this through various examples. Here again, we can make bring math closer to actual experience. Draw 12 dots in 2 rows of 6. Then, using different colored pencils circle 2 groups of 6, 3 groups of 4 and 6 groups of 2. A small circle around each dot may be drawn first as well as a large circle around the whole. An arrow to each circle may be used to label the grouping: 12 divided by 1 is 12; 12 divided by 2 is 6; 12 divided by 3 is 4; 12 divided by 6 is 2; 12 divided by 12 is 1.

By dividing the 12 sticks into 4 square pens the division begins. Raymond is able to guess the divisions because he is already familiar with some of his times tables, in this case his 3s.

HER HIGHNESS MINUS (p.26)

Here, too, a character embodies a mathematical process. Queen Hellene, 'Her Highness Minus', is a generous figure. She lends a different perspective to 'taking away' through 'giving away'.

Illustration: Draw a picture of the queen holding out her hand. Emphasize that the outstretched fingers. Elsewhere draw the minus sign artistically with a nice background and contrasting colors.

GIVING AWAY IN A FAST WAY (pp.27-28)

This chapter illustrates the relationship between subtraction and division, one similar to that between addition and multiplication. In both cases the process is speeded up. Raymond deepens his understanding of division. Again his familiarity with multiplication helps him understand. Multiplicando wisely gives a very simple illustration in order to make the process clear.

Illustration: The illustration of the pantry on page 27, with numbers prominently written, gives a strong image for 3 goes into 30 ten times. Alternate stories could equally well be used. For example, there could be a pirates cave with sacks of booty, say 12. Three pirates go into the cave to remove the sacks and heft them 'above ground'. Even if they only take one at a time, in the end each will have removed 4 from the cave. This may be acted out, even with a bit of pushing and shoving from the pirates, Argh! Here, too, someone draws a sketch of the scene.

CHECKING (pp.29-30)

Part of learning the times tables and their relation to division is developing a feel for the sound of 'number families', combinations of 3 numbers. Reciting in this way is a path to mastery through hearing.

Say the related numbers; say the multiplication fact; then say it right to left replacing 'is' with the division sign, and replacing the times sign with 'is' (column 3).

Say 3 4 12, 3 X 4 is 12. Then reverse it, 12 ÷ 4 is 3.

Raymond recognizes the relation between the multiplication table and finding the correct answer in division problems. Rosemary reinforces for Raymond the importance of memorizing the multiplication facts. It's better that she does it rather than the teacher!

Multiplicando and King Divide refer to themselves brothers, thus metaphorically restating the connection between dividing and multiplying.

Raymond's saying "I almost understand" reflects what I call the 'percolation effect" in learning, understanding being a gradual process of recognition.

DOUBLE THREES (p.31)

Doing "double 3s" requires mastery of 3s. Say the 3s, emphasizing every other number beginning with 6. As Raymond observes, it does get harder once 36 is passed. If need be, to avoid fatigue, one can begin on 36+3, or 39.

A good beginning to mastering the 6s may be made by referring to the 3s table. By noting every other 3s fact, the 6s become visible. Hence, 6 is <u>2</u>X3,   12 is <u>4</u>X3,   18 is <u>6</u>X3...   By copying the 3s with the even multipliers we have half the Table of Sixes already completed.

Here it may be shown that multiplying any number by 2, doubling it, will result in an even number. Thus, every other 3 is in the 6 table. Show 3 fingers on one hand and then match 3 from the other hand to them. This is a very graphic demonstration of this simple principle.

DOUBLE FOURS (pp.32-35)

The similarity between double 3s and double 4s is fairly obvious. As with the 6s, we find the first half of the 8s table in the 4s table. Here we can introduce the notion that adding 8s is like adding 10 and subtracting 2. Thus the number in the ones column keeps falling by 2. Say as if it is a rhyme:

"8+10 is 18. Give away 2 is 16.

16+10 is 26. Give away 2 is 24

24 +10 is 34. Give away 2 is 32... Observe the pattern and hear it.

Step up to eight. This is the same principle as the 48 Club, except counting by 2s. Thus, we step up on 2, with the other foot on 4, step down with one foot on 6, and with the other foot and clap on 8, and so on.

The 9s harken back to the 3s, except this time we skip to the third number. It is fitting as we counted in this way to derive the 3s from the 1s. Here, too, much can be learned from observing the pattern. As Raymond points out, "the ones column drops down by one each time while the tens column goes up. We could use the same activity as above, adding 10 and giving away 1. After all, 9 is 10-1. Try saying: 9 +10 is 19. Give away 1 is 18.

18+10 is 28. Give away 1 is 27.   27+10 is 37. Give away 1 is 36.

WAYS OF SAYING (p.36)

Here is an opportunity to broaden the definitions of the four processes. Find as many examples as you can and discuss them with the children. Make four quadrants and label them, and put the different ways of saying under the rubric.

ROSEMARY DREAMS ELEVEN (pp.37-38)

Rosemary's dream is quite self-explanatory. With 11 we are adding 10+1 each time. Hence, 10 and 1, 20+2 30+3...

Illustration: In drawing the vases et al. it might be preferable to line them up in vertical columns on a table, a bit more comfortable for adding.

We only go to 99, 9X11. How would you find 10, 11 and 12X11?

SAME WITH TWELVES, A LITTLE DIFFERENT (p.39)

The title speaks for itself. Instead of adding 10+1 we are adding 10+2. The procedure is the same as with 11s.

MULTIPLICANDO'S TABLE (pp.40-41)

The story comes full circle. The children experience the magnificence of Multiplicando's Table, now having mastered it. Multiplicando must leave the children, but what he has taught them will remain. The magic of the nines presages further discoveries in mathematics.

To demonstrate the magic of 9, begin by making a colorful card for each of the numerals 0-9. Have 10 children line up in order horizontally across the room holding a card at chest level. At a signal from the teacher the children on either end of the line, 0 and 9, peel off, meeting in the middle. There they hold their cards above their heads while they say "9". Next, 1 and 8 step in front of them making/saying "18". Now 2 and 7 stand in front of them saying "27", followed by 3 and 6 (36), and 4 and 5 (45). Next, 4 and 5 exchange places while taking a step forward (54). 3 and 6 now do the same (63), followed by 7 and 2 (72), 8 and 1 (81) and 9 and 0 (90), each pair saying its "name". Having accomplished this, on a signal from the teacher, 9 and 0 return to their original places. When they get there they hold up their cards while the class says, "0+9=9". Likewise, 1 and 8 return to their original positions and hold up their cards while the class says, "1+8=9". The same is done with 2+7=9, 3+6=9, and 4+5=9. Now that all numerals are in their places they continue holding up their cards at the appropriate times while the class says, 5+4=9, 6+3=9, 7+2=9, 8+1=9, and 9+0=9. To complete the presentation of 9 do a wave 1-9 and back down to 1. Perhaps 0 could bow, and then the other numbers follow suit, just to add a little humor.

*This activity may also be used to demonstrate the 9s table. Here the class would state the multiplication fact represented by the particular numerals being held up. Thus, 9 is 1X9, 18 is 2X9, 27 is 3X9, 36 is 4X9, 45 is 5X9, 54 is 6X9, 63 is 7X9, 72 is 8X9, 81 is 9X9 and 90 is 10X9.

www.ingramcontent.com/pod-product-compliance
Lightning Source LLC
Chambersburg PA
CBHW042032150426
43200CB00002B/29